WHAT PEOPLE A

Way of the I

Flavia's words will make you fee   ﹐ᴜy and magic of the faery realm all over again. Voices from childhood return, and I feel the urge to clap... these aren't just the pretty sprites of the Victorians but true tales of the land, beautifully told, in all their Puckish wildness.
Cat Treadwell, druid priestess and author of *Facing the Darkness.*

My inspiration comes from my love of nature and fascination for ancient legend, just as Flavia's words of guidance in this book do. We both agree 'Fae' represents the natural world we live in, and now more than ever, it is a communion with this world that we must cultivate and respect in order to once again bring about the real beauty in humanity.
Linda Ravenscroft, world renowned fairy & fantasy artist.

Flavia walks her talk, her passion for the Fae is as real as it gets and in world that needs more magic Flavia brings just that. I love her honest heartfelt approach, the Fae worlds shine through her.
David Wells, astrologer, presenter and author of *Your Astrological Moon Sign: Werewolf, Angel, Vampire, Saint? - Discover Your Hidden Inner Self.*

Flavia has an intuitive connection to the faery realms. She speaks in a way that is easy for all to understand, and makes communication with the Fae effortless. This book should be on the shelves of every faery lover as a treasured reference for those treading a faery path for years to come.
Karen Kay, Editor in Chief, FAE Magazine.

Way of the Faery Shaman

The book of spells, incantations,
meditations & faery magic

Shaman Pathways

Way of the Faery Shaman

The book of spells, incantations,
meditations & faery magic

Flavia Kate Peters

MOON
BOOKS

Winchester, UK
Washington, USA

First published by Moon Books, 2014
Moon Books is an imprint of John Hunt Publishing Ltd., Laurel House, Station Approach,
Alresford, Hants, SO24 9JH, UK
office1@jhpbooks.net
www.johnhuntpublishing.com
www.moon-books.net

For distributor details and how to order please visit the 'Ordering' section on our website.

Text copyright: Flavia Kate Peters 2014

ISBN: 978 1 78279 905 4

A CIP catalogue record for this book is available from the British Library.

Design: Stuart Davies
www.stuartdaviesart.com

Cover image: Linda Ravenscroft

Printed and bound by CPI Group (UK) Ltd, Croydon, CR0 4YY

We operate a distinctive and ethical publishing philosophy in all
areas of our business, from our global network of authors to
production and worldwide distribution.

CONTENTS

Dedication

For the Fae... with my love

Foreword

The most magical time of my life was as a little girl, in the Scottish Highlands, engaged in the old stories of how Faery Doctors, wise men and women, specially chosen by the Fae, lived and worked with them. Working with faeries was one of the earliest forms of ritual magic and healing, which was honoured and revered in an oral tradition.

Shamanism is humankind's most primal form of connection to both the spirit of the land, and the elements of nature. Faery Shamans have the ability to connect to the elements, all of nature and the faery realms of the Four Directions. The Faery Shaman grows with seasons, recognises the call of the wilds and the change of the winds. In these crucial times of climate change and destruction of this precious planet, the Faery World urges us to walk the way of the Faery Shaman.

Flavia Kate Peters reveals how we can once again restore the mysterious and magical path of the Faery Shaman into our lives. The world of nature is waiting for the Faery Shamans to reawaken and reclaim a world of magic, which is easily accessed through the pages of this book.

Barbara Meiklejohn-Free, The Highland Seer and bestselling author of *The Shaman Within*.

Introduction

Brilliant, you heard them! You answered the call of the faeries. They knew you could do it. But why have they called you specifically? Well, you actually know the answer to that, deep in your soul. But allow, if you will, the magic of these pages to remind you. For you are invited to re-discover the truth of who the faeries really are, and work with the forces of nature through spell work, through meditation, invocation and rhyme.

You will embrace the elements that actually govern us, here on our beloved planet. Your senses will heighten as you grow more sensitive to every aspect of the natural world and its magic. By working and living each day this way, the faeries will assist in enhancing your natural magical abilities, heal your spiritual, physical and emotional wellbeing and bring you back to a real connection to the Elemental Realm.

Romantic notions of fairy tales and magical beings of 'make believe' abound, which mostly stem from pictures such as the Cottingley Fairies of the 1800s to the enchanting beings created by Walt Disney, like Ariel the Little Mermaid, Tinker Bell and Cinderella's Fairy Godmother, we are no strangers to fairy dust, magic wands, and fairy rings!

However, faeries are far from the sparkling characters of children's bed-time stories; they are very real beings of nature and are as magical and as old as the hills. Written mention of Faeries such as nymphs, satyrs and fauns are found in the texts of Homer's Iliad and Odyssey. In the days of Ancient Greece, gods and goddesses were worshipped and minor deities were recognised as the spirits of nature. Faeries were honoured in the waters, meadows, forests and flowers…

Where round the bed, whence Achelous springs, that wat'ry Fairies dance in mazy rings. Iliad, B. xxiv. 617.
What sounds are those that gather from the shores, the voice of nymphs

that haunt the sylvan bowers, the fair-hair'd dryads of the shady wood, or azure daughters of the silver flood? Odyssey, B. vi. 122.

The early Roman religion understood we shared our homes with household spirits and guardians, and flying faeries played a part in Oriental, Arabian and Asian cultures. Ancient Norse traditions include stories of elves, Lorelei and other such beings of magical folklore, and faeries were found from the Scottish faery mounds of the Sidhe, to the Tuatha De Danaan of Irish barrows.

Like in many other cultures, the ancient Celts made faeries an important part of everyday life. For these beings of nature were treated with a deep reverence. It was general protocol to leave small gifts of food or milk as a mark of respect and gratitude. Our ancestors knew that faeries had the power to bestow them with a bountiful harvest, or cause destruction to the entire crop. It was believed that elves spread diseases and if someone was ill they were said to be 'fairy taken'.

Faeries were also accused of stealing babies, often in return for a fairy child that was left in its place. These were called Changelings and were often spotted by having an unusual 'Fae' appearance or of something different to the original child. Through the superstitious ages of the Anglo-Saxons, when a baby became sick it was believed that it had become a Changeling, and many an innocent baby was burned to death in order to get rid of this 'evil being' said to have been put in its place. People wanted to protect themselves from these types of encounters and so never an ill word was spoken of the spirits of nature.

However, faeries were seen as beings with supernatural powers, as magical beings, and were often sought after for help and assistance in finding items, healing and cures, seeing the future and other good wishes. In these times people would seek out the wise man or woman of the community, the cunning man or cunning woman or a Faery Doctor. These people had the ability to connect with the magic of the Elemental Realm and heal, with the assistance of these beings.

During the time of Queen Elizabeth I of England, the playwright William Shakespeare (1564-1616) popularised faeries in his play A Midsummer Night's Dream. Before him, Chaucer (1342-1400) indicated that Britain was a land filled with faeries before the times of the great King Arthur. British Arthurian legends tell of magic, sorcery and faery half-breeds such as Arthur's half-sister Morgan Le Fay (meaning and deriving from the French word 'Faery'), and the part-mortal magician, Merlin..

However, when Christianity reached fever-pitch, during the Middle-Ages, faeries were accused of being fallen angels, and demons. Interestingly the Greek word for spirit is 'Daimon', and therefore cleverly used by the power of suggestion that these beings were works of the relatively new-invented 'Satan'. The gruesome times of the Witch-hunts of the 1400s-1600s made sure that no-one conversed with the magic of nature or the faeries themselves.

The natural seers and healers were accused of working with, and for, 'evil', and thousands of innocent men and women were killed in the name of 'good' across Europe. Murderously the worship of nature was stamped out, or so these pagan-fearing hunters thought.

Disconnection with human-kind encouraged the faeries to go 'underground', so to speak, until the Victorian era. This was the time of the Industrial Revolution when the land was being raped in the name of 'progress'. Railway tracks were being laid, rivers and streams were dammed and the air was filled with heavy pollution for the first time.

The Nature Spirits needed us to hear their plight and so faeries came back into the minds and hearts of those who could sense them. Sadly by this time many a man's heart was corrupted by centuries of disempowerment, and the death in the belief in magic. Today this is still pretty much the consensus; however there do seem to be more people turning to accepting that

Faeries are real, and a new train of thought is changing the way that faeries are perceived.

For many, faeries are now deemed to be wearing stripy tights, covered in glitter, spreading fairy dust as they flit around granting wishes with their shiny wands. Faery festivals and balls are popping up all around the UK, Europe and the USA, and the faeries are being honoured through costume, dance and movement. At these events you could mistake the party revellers for actual faeries themselves. For they blend into nature beautifully in wearing hand-made outfits and masks made of leaves and flowers, whilst donning pointy ears.

Perhaps these are the faeries of old, appearing now in human form - for remember that previous lifetimes are spent in many different realms! It is wonderful that in this lifetime those who feel a connection with the magic and mystery of the Faery Realm can stand proudly and publicly, whilst fun and laughter are enjoyed. Joy, after all, is the highest vibration and a much sought-after gift of the Fae, but what of the 'real' Elemental Realm?

It is not to be toyed with for it is filled with many a gnarled creature who is disgruntled. As I write this I am given an image of a being, with the look of wood, wandering through a darkened pathway of trees with decaying leaves rotting underfoot, covered by a canopy of entwined branches up above. But through the golden stalks of wheat, meadows filled with wild flowers and grasses, plays out a different kind of faery - of golden light, exuding joy.

There are many avenues of the Faery Realm to be explored and honoured through ritual, invocation and incantation. Seek out the magic within and the magic around you will surely show itself.

The Earth needs your help and the Fae are calling you to harness the power of nature. In return they offer you their assistance to enable you to thrive in this very modern world, in balance and harmony, and with a sprinkle of real magic.

Their invitation is in your hands...

Chapter 1

Following the Faery Path

My first recollection of faeries was during a hot summer's day when I was two years old. My father was taking part in a cricket match and I was playing with other children at the edge of the village green. There stood a huge oak tree, which had a hollow doorway at the base of its trunk. As I peered up I saw tiny twinkling lights darting about and I called out. An older boy came along pushing me out of the way. As he stared up through the darkness he shouted 'I can see faeries!'

A year later my family moved to a house surrounded by vast woodland and there I spent my childhood peering through any hole or hollow that I could find in the trees, looking for faeries. As the years went by I had built up an amazing relationship with these magical beings having spent hours in the woods talking to the faeries, communing and connecting with them, and learning from the nature that surrounded me.

As part of my spiritual journey I was guided to California to train to become an Angel Therapist with renowned angel lady and author, Doreen Virtue PhD. The training location was stunning. The grounds were filled with the most beautiful flowers and plants that decorated pathways which led to the golden sands that lined the Pacific Ocean - Heaven on Earth!

As I was taking a stroll to the beach I felt led to smell some delicate white flowers to the left of me. Suddenly, I felt compelled to ask permission to breathe in their scent and immediately heard a small voice saying 'Yes, do so.' Well, I was rather surprised and stood there stunned for a moment. I heard a voice again asking 'Well, will you?' So obediently I leant forward and stuck my nose in and breathed up the heavenly scent. 'Thank you,' I said feeling something on my nose. Careful not to hurt whatever it was, I tried to gently brush it away, but to no avail.

The next day in class we were asked to get into pairs. I coupled with a pretty petite lady, with long curly brown hair. She introduced herself and then exclaimed 'You have a faery on your nose. She's pink!'

When I returned home, I set about building up my Angel Practice. I asked the angels to help me find a suitable place to work from and was guided to an ideal shop in my local town, which had a large spacious room at the side of the building. It was a faery shop and was run by a lady named Twinkle. I was able to run angel workshops, meditation groups and give angel readings and healings comfortably. I also helped out, when I could, selling faery items and all things sparkly.

As client numbers grew I had no choice but to look for bigger premises, which didn't take long. Within days I was led to a Wellbeing Centre that had tranquil therapy rooms and the most exquisite covered courtyard, filled with plants and flowers. Liz Graham was the owner and she welcomed me with open arms. The place was perfect and so I signed up to continue my Angel Therapies from there.

One day, as I was at the Centre, deciding on dates for more angel workshops, I suddenly heard the stamping of tiny feet and voices crying, 'What about us!' It was the faeries. I felt terrible. How could I have not even thought about running faery workshops? They need to be heard; they need to be believed in!

So I consciously agreed with the faeries to be their representative. I enlisted their help so that they could give me the information that they wanted me to get across to others. I found that we worked very easily together. This led me to run faery events throughout the UK for adults and children alike, as well as writing articles and meditations for Mind Body Spirit publications including the faery press.

Faeries are all around us, but it is just that we, as humans, are usually unable to readily see them. They belong to our physical world and also their realm, known as the Ether, the Otherworld or Faerieland, which is hidden within our world.

Faeries resonates at a higher energy frequency than ours, which is why it is difficult for humans, who are of a heavy dense energy, to see, but they can freely visit both worlds as they are made up of high vibrating energy of light. At certain times of the day, such as the magical hours of Sunrise, Dusk, Noon and Midnight, we are more likely to connect with, and see, faeries. Portals from this world to theirs exist through water pools, at the crossings of ancient paths and from circles of mushrooms or flowers. Here we are more able to see them in our physical world - if we are lucky!

Faeries are able to slow their vibrations down purposefully if they wish to appear to us. This happened to me whilst I was giving a faery workshop one Saturday in the beautiful courtyard at the Wellbeing Centre. Two large faeries, who, incidentally, had incredibly long legs, turned up just as I was connecting the participants with the energy of a faery ring. They both hovered in the air to the right of the group, who were in a meditative state. As I looked at the Fae visitors silently I asked why they had appeared. They replied that they just wanted to see what was 'going on'. I told them that they were welcome.

To earn their trust, faeries will look to see if we have done unselfish deeds for the environment, such as pick up trash, be kind to animals and recycling. If we haven't, then they might set us tasks. Usually this is to collect dropped litter left in nature. If you walk past an empty drink can or candy wrapper, for example, and suddenly feel compelled to pick it up, you can be sure that the faeries are testing you.

Go for it, this will build up trust and kick-start off a wonderful new relationship between yourself and the fairies. The more you follow their guidance, in this way, the more natural it will become. The faeries will always show you their appreciation, in some way or another - just look for the signs!

I was walking through a park that is visible to a busy town roundabout. As I looked down I noticed broken green glass on the lawn that could be a potential hazard for animals. I bent down to pick up the glass pieces and took them to the nearest bin, which was quite a walk away. As I continued with this ritual, which took a good 20 minutes, I endured shouts from passing cars, and horn blowing, as if I was doing something quite mad. I just smiled, and returned no judgment.

I was pleased to put the last few pieces in the bin, and as I looked toward a cherry tree, I saw a leprechaun materialise in front of me. He was dressed all in green, including his hat, and was about 2 - 3 feet tall. With a knowing nod, he disappeared just as quickly as he'd arrived. I just knew that he was acknowledging me for what I had just done.

Faeries may not always make themselves visually apparent. You may feel the presence of faeries through a change of energy, such as a feeling of euphoria or you might feel a physical push or prod.

Often faeries dance on the top of people's heads, this may feel quite spidery, so be careful not to knock them off if it tickles! They might leave you a gift, such as a stone or a crystal. A book may jump out at you; you may overhear a relevant conversation or receive a faery related gift from a friend.

If you, and the faeries, feel that you have a good relationship then they will immediately set to work to bring you what you desire (for the highest good of all, of course) - all you have to do is be clear about what you want and to ask. And remember the phrase 'be careful what you wish for!'

Faeries can assist us with our material concerns. They are brilliant manifestors, meaning they know how to attract or create dreams and make them a reality, as this is what they do naturally. They remind us of the importance of staying focused on, and positive about, our desires.

If you need your financial life healed, or an abundant flow of prosperity, for instance, then you can count your lucky stars that you are friends with the faeries. All they do is imagine what they want and it is created for them in an instant. For example, they may picture themselves with a big cream cake - and 'hey presto' a big cream cake appears!

The faeries tell us that we actually do the same. Whatever we think transforms into reality in the Ether, the Otherworld. Then it is through asking for assistance, and taking guided action that we can bring, with the faeries' help, our dreams into reality.

Remember to be careful what you are imagining though, as the faeries have access to what we are seeing in our minds. Sometimes it's fun to play with the faeries in this way - for example, you could imagine yourself with very pointy pixie ears and a long, long nose and they will see you in this way instantly.

The faeries love this kind of play and will laugh! It's a great way to build up a relationship with the faeries for they enjoy laughter and playing with the magical energies that are all around us.

So because of the faeries' magical abilities to create what they desire we too can call upon the faeries to assist us! I was given this exact information during a healing session, as I was guided to see, in my mind's eye, the client's ailment as perfectly whole and healed. I realised that this was how the faeries live and bring about all that they desire, and so I decided to work with them in this way.

I had been invited to attend a faery ball in Cornwall, which was about a 5 hour drive from where I lived. I longed to go and join in such fun! Having a lean month financially I was concerned about paying for accommodation and the cost of fuel to travel. So, I visualized it all as happening and asked the faeries to assist in my desire.

I then felt guided to buy a Lotto scratch card (which I don't ever usually do!) But the feeling was so strong that I couldn't ignore it and so I went ahead. In the shop I scanned my eyes over the many choices until I saw the words 'Lucky Leprechaun', which of course I chose.

Back at home I was putting the key into the lock of my front door and from the flower beds to my left I heard the cheesiest words used in all the best fairy-tale stories, 'You shall go to the ball!' I raced indoors and lit a small faery candle and sat crossed legged in front of it, with the words still echoing through my mind. With a coin I carefully scratched off the silver coating of the scratch card, to reveal three green shamrocks... I had won a hundred pounds!

That would pay for petrol and food for my trip away. How wonderful, but what of accommodation? With that, a text message appeared on my mobile phone, from the organiser of the event, inviting me to stay with her, for that period of time, in a delightful cottage overlooking the Cornish coast with no charge!

As the faeries had proven to me, working with and trusting in their ability to provide is a powerful way to create our lives. I always leave a token of my appreciation in return for any assistance they have given me, such as a piece of bread and honey, a glass of mead or some chocolate, which the faeries consume by breathing in the essence of the offering, rather than taking it physically. You will always know when a faery has accepted and 'taken' the gift, noticing that the life force energy of the food or beverage has completely disappeared..

The faeries are indeed very real and are waiting to share with us the magic that exists within and all around us. They reveal the beauty and power of our inner-selves and assist us with magical solutions and insights to situations, if we just but ask.

We can connect with the faeries at any time - especially when we are relaxed in nature or meditating. So invite the faeries in and allow them to help you to shine...

Connecting with the Faery Realm Meditation

Find a quiet spot where you won't be disturbed - preferably outside, or next to a plant or crystal. Breathing steadily, see yourself surrounded by an iridescent ball of rainbow light, which protects you fully with angel energy. With your eyes closed, take three deep breaths and then let your breath remain deep, but steady.

As you continue to breathe, you begin to sense a smell - something quite familiar - what is it? You know this scent; you recognize it - but can't quite grasp it. You know it is from memories long, long ago. Something comforting, safe, but also wonderful - something that you connect with at the deepest level.

And then in your mind's eye you find that you are sitting against a huge, strong tree in a grassy glade. Your back leans against the rough bark and you feel the spongy green moss beneath you. You can hear the beautiful song of birds...

As you look around, you see mighty, majestic trees surrounding the glade - see the bright green of their leaves as the sunlight streams through them. It is beautiful and you notice that as these shafts of bright golden light shine through the trees, they meet together, as one blast of blinding light, in the clearing just in front of you. Your eyes squint at the brightness, but you cannot take your eyes off this sight - it's like nature's own treasure chest of gold!

The light is getting larger and brighter and expands out, getting nearer and nearer to you - you feel more and more comforted, more and more at peace and you just know that this is the light of the Divine, the light of the Mother coming to nurture you and to fill you with her goodness.

Breathe in the light... feel it fill your heart... feel your heart expand like a flower opening... breathe this pure light energy in, as it fills your body - all the way down through the legs, into the feet and out of the soles of your feet, into the ground, deep into the Earth. Instantly you feel a connection with the energy of the Earth, the Earth magic mixing with the light that is now within you and part of you.

Breathe this new energy up. Feel it as you draw it up in through your feet, up your legs - feel the surge as it rushes to fill your entire body, breathe it in as this amazing light cleanses every cell, every vessel... moving on up through the throat, moving through your face, filling your head and bursting out of your crown at the top your head - up and up - reaching to the highest levels of love ...

Feel and see the light expanding, showering down on you. Beautiful light of protection, love and magic energy, filling you, surrounding you and connecting you to All. Bathe in this glorious light, soaking in the Divine energy - feeling every part of you coming alive. As the sun moves round, the shafts of light become hidden from the trees and your eyes adjust slowly. You are beginning to see the woodland that you are sitting in.

Just there you see some movement, a spark of light - no, two or three - no, more, many more... sparkling orbs, dancing in and out of the trees - and with a rub of your eyes, you see in front of you 'tiny' folk - yes faeries! But 'oh' also elves and other beings who have come to greet you! So many of them, all approaching - some smiling and some looking very shy - and you realize that you are sitting in the heart of the faeries' ring!

Take some time to be introduced and then introduce yourself. Open your heart, so that they know they can trust you. Find out what these magical beings have come to tell you - what do they want you to know? What would you like to tell them? What would you like their help with? Listen well to their response on all levels. One of your new friends whispers their name and another puts something in your hand.

Dusk is falling, and you feel a chill - it is time for you to come back and so you say your goodbyes. You feel such joy, such amazement that you have just connected with the Faerie Realm;

you have been chosen as a faerie confidante and you know that you can connect with these new friends any time, for they will always be there for you.

But how are you able to leave this place of magic and wonder? And then it comes to you, quite clearly... you breathe... deeply... taking a deep inhale and exhale, inhale and exhale, inhale... and gently open your eyes.

Welcome back!

Chapter 2

Elements and Elementals

The faeries urge us to be their voice; they are calling us to be the ambassadors of nature and help heal and clean up this beautiful planet.

The Faery Realm is made up of many beings such as gnomes, elves, dwarfs, leprechauns, fauns, flower faeries, mermaids, fire spirits, pixies and many more. Each faery 'type' is assigned to, and belongs in, the category of one of the four basic elements - Earth, Air, Fire and Water.

Each element is necessary for human life, and without them this planet would be lifeless. The elements work in harmony, even though at times it can seem otherwise, to create and to sustain life.

The elementals are the faery guardians of a specific element, of one of the basic four, and their task is to literally make that element work. They are the power behind the elements. This is why faery beings are known as 'elementals', a name given by the Swiss alchemist, Paracelsus, in the Middle Ages.

The basic four elements and all of nature cannot exist without the workings from the Faery Kingdom, for they are the root of all existing matter. The elements are the physical manifestations of the faeries existence made manifest from the Ethers, the Otherworld, Faery Land. Each element has a principle elemental 'guardian' from the Faery Realm...

Gnomes

Gnomes are the guardians of the element of Earth. These are the nature spirits who toil away at the soil, sifting through it in order for the nourishment to be at its best, enabling the plants to grow and for certain insect species to live in. Without the help of the

Gnomes, we would have no plants or trees, no fruits, vegetables or salads to eat. The Gnomes provide us with a place to reside, to call our home. Sadly their job today is a thankless and difficult task. Due to humans' abuse of the land from extensive farming and the use of pesticides and other chemicals, the Gnomes have to work their magic that much harder because of the depletion of minerals from the Earth.

It is always wonderful when people place faery artefacts into their gardens, especially as 'like attracts like'. This means that faeries will always come to see and be near statues of themselves and this is a good way to encourage them into your back (or front) yard. I am always bemused and slightly concerned, however, when I walk past houses or bungalows and see colourful statues of garden gnomes perfectly placed upon concreted paved-over gardens, with not a hint of soil in sight! It totally contradicts the Gnome's very task!

Earth Faery Magic

- Zodiac - Capricorn, Taurus and Virgo.
- Season - Winter
- Direction - North
- Magical Time - Midnight
- Candle Colour - Brown or Black
- Elemental - Gnome

Sylphs

The guardians of the element of Air are the Sylphs. These are the wispy, whispering faeries who bring messages through the winds. If you look up into the skies and re-adjust your eyes you can see them as tiny pin-pricks of light, dancing in the breeze. The Sylphs' role is to purify the air, so that all loving beings that walk and grow on the Earth can breathe easily. Without these faeries of Air we could not exist.

Sadly they too have to work their magic harder than ever as

the air becomes more and more polluted these days with car exhaust and factory fumes, methane gas emissions and even nuclear explosions!

We can help the Sylphs out by visualising Divine white light spreading through the skies, eliminating smoke, smog and pollution in order to clean up and purify the air. Remember that whatever we imagine is seen, and takes action in the Etheric World, thus manifesting into this world.

Air Faery Magic

- Zodiac - Aquarius, Gemini, Libra
- Season - Spring
- Direction - East
- Magical Time - Dawn
- Candle Colour - Yellow
- Elemental - Sylph

Salamanders

The guardians of Fire are the Salamanders. They exist in the Etheric World until they are summoned to this earthly existence by the form of a matchstick, a lighter or an electrical appliance. Salamanders are lizard like in appearance, of red, orange and yellow and can be seen within the shapes of flames - no fire can exist without them!

Their electrical counterparts are white, violet and pale blue in colour, and are often forgotten when we boil the kettle, switch on a light or use the oven. Every time we use an electrical appliance we are communing and working with Salamanders.

Of all the elemental guardians these are probably the most feared, but actually should not be! For if you work with these fiery beings, and respect them and the fire they create, then they will protect you, your loved ones and possessions from the ravishing effects of fire itself.

Fire Faery Magic

- Zodiac - Aries, Leo, Sagittarius
- Season - Summer
- Direction - South
- Magical Time - Noon
- Candle colour - Red
- Elemental - Salamander

Undines

The guardians of Water are the Undines. These are the nature spirits of wherever water exists such as the lakes, rivers, pools, wells, oceans and even the rain itself. The Undines' role is to nurture and protect the animals and plants that reside in these bodies of waters, as well as the water itself.

Every time you take a shower or relax in a hot bath, you have the opportunity to commune with the Undines and to utilise their powers. Each time we drink a glass of water we are taking their energies into ourselves and communing with the Undines on a sub-conscious level. The Undines work closely with the Sylphs of the Air when it comes to a westerly, wet wind and also with the Salamanders of Fire during an electrical storm.

The Undines are fighting to keep the oceans clean and clear of pollution from shipping as well as from eroding soil during rainstorms. Much of this runoff flows to the sea, carrying with it agricultural fertilizers and pesticides.

Eighty percent of pollution to the marine environment comes from small sources from the land such as septic tanks and motor oil. We can help the Undines by taking physical measures to stop the pollution by supporting clean up groups such as Oceana.org and/or by visualising clean and pure waters across the globe.

You are invited to perform a spell for this very work later on in the 'The Magic of Water' chapter of this book.

Water Faery Magic

- Zodiac - Pisces, Cancer, Scorpio
- Season - Autumn
- Direction - West
- Magical Time - Dusk
- Candle Colour - Blue
- Elemental – Undines

Protection and Grounding

The exciting thing about the Faery World is that we can literally work with the elementals and bring their magic into this realm! In faery magic the elements can be called upon for specific spells. Each element of Earth, Air, Fire and Water is joined but the fifth etheric element of Spirit, which runs through everything that is alive, including the elements. The combined five elements are represented in the magical ancient symbol of a five-pointed star - the pentagram.

Putting a circle around the star is protective of the five elements and the magical user, and is called the Pentacle. Ancient wise men and women, witches and magical practitioners used this sacred symbol for casting spells (for the highest good) and protection for centuries until sadly it became seen as a sign of evil and Satanism. As you will have read in the 'Introduction' of this book, this was to stamp out empowerment, in favour of control. I can assure you that the Pentacle is a sign of good, of connection with nature and the natural magic that we are part of.

Whenever we do any magical work it is vitally important that we protect ourselves. In fact it is good practise to call in protection every day, whether we are consciously working with the Spirit World, or not.

Before partaking in any work with Spirit, be it meditation, invocation or any other form, you must 'ground' yourself. This is so that you are anchored, within your body, and are kept connected to this Earth realm. You may wish to call upon the

Gnomes, the Earth elementals, for their assistance with this. Going outside, into nature, and standing barefooted on the ground will instantly ground and connect you to the Earth.

Or, wherever you are, imagine strong roots growing down from the soles of your feet burying deep into the ground. See, in your mind's eye, your roots growing stronger and longer until they reach the centre of the Earth.

Now visualise a huge crystal. Take notice of what it looks like and allow your roots to wrap around it. Now breathe up the crystalline energy, breathe up the Earth magic and allow it to surge through every cell, every vessel, and every part of your very being. You are now grounded, and ready to connect.

In my experience the Pentacle is the strongest form of protection. It guards you against unwanted energies from other people, such as psychic attacks, negative thought forms and from locations, such as old buildings.

In order to connect with the Elemental Realm, and the world of Spirit, it is important to be a clear channel, which means being free of negativity and fear. Simply imagining the Pentacle surrounding you will immediately give you the protection that is required.

Other ways include; visualising the pentagram in front of you, see it growing to the size of you and then step into it. Draw a Pentacle in the air with your power finger, (the index finger of your dominant hand) in front of you, above you, below you, at both sides and behind you. Or you may wish to use the following visualisation which will ground, centre and protect you before taking up any magical work…

Protection, Grounding and Centring Ceremony

Stand, feet slightly apart, but firmly on the ground. See, in your mind's eye, your roots (as explained above) growing deeply into the Earth below you and allow them to anchor. Feel the strong and grounding Earth energy as you connect with the guardians of the element of Earth, the Gnomes.

You become aware of a soft breeze caressing your body as the guardians of Air, the Sylphs, surround you. Breathe in the air deeply. Feel and welcome this precious life-giver as it enters your lungs. You become aware of a light, refreshing rain landing upon you. Embrace the guardians of Water, the Undines, who have come to cleanse and purify you.

A fluffy white cloud moves in the sky, to reveal the Sun in all its glory. The guardians of Fire, the Salamanders, beat down their burning rays upon you. Feel the delicious warmth, nurturing and healing your body.

With the power of all four elements connecting with every part of you, feel yourself merge with each one of them. Now draw on the strength of this energy, feel the power surge through every part of you as you raise your arms. Stand like a star and become the pentagram as your feel your spirit soar. You are the Earth, the Air, the Fire, the Water and Spirit. Now see yourself circled with a protective energy as you become the Pentacle. You are now grounded, centred and fully protected.

The exciting thing about the Faery World is that we can work with the elementals and bring their magic into this realm! In faery magic the elements can be called upon for specific spells. Each element of Earth, Air, Fire and Water is joined but the fifth Etheric element of Spirit, which runs through everything that is alive, including the elements.

Each element is represented in the magical ancient symbol of a five pointed star, the pentagram. Putting a circle around the star is protective of the five elements and the magical user, and is called the Pentacle.

Ancient wise men and women, witches and magical practitioners used this sacred symbol for casting spells (for the highest good) and protection for centuries until sadly it became seen as a sign of evil and Satanism. As mentioned, this was to quash empowerment to gain control. The Pentacle is a sign of good, of connection with nature and the real magic that we are part of. If you feel drawn to honour and work with the magical spirit of nature then creating an altar is the perfect way to do so.

Creating a Faery Magic Altar

An altar doesn't have to be anything grand, so don't worry if you don't have the room! It can be a table with a cloth on it in a quiet corner, a mantel, a window sill or bathroom shelf. It doesn't matter so long as you have set the right intention.

Once you have found your perfect altar you will need to find items to represent each element. A pentagram is always a good idea to keep on your altar, which can be in the form of a pendant, a picture or why not make one with sticks? You will need the following...

To represent Earth - A bowl of soil from your homeland or a sacred site. White Californian sage (this is cleansing and purifying when lit and can count towards the Fire element too). Crystals and stones.

To represent Fire - A candle (the lit flame). A symbol or representation of the Sun.

To represent Air - A lit incense stick. Feathers (preferable retrieved fallen feathers found in nature). Bells. Wind chimes.

To represent Water - Water from a holy place (such as Glastonbury Chalice Well). A chalice/ goblet (to represent the Water element or to hold the water itself). Sea shells.

I usually adorn my altar with small faery figurines, including dragons and mermaids. You may wish to stand a picture or two of an elemental being, the woods, a meadow, the ocean and scatter pine cones or leaves over the surface. Build whatever you feel represents the magic of nature for you. By including all four elements/elementals on your altar ensures the balance in all aspects of nature, when honouring or doing all round spell work.

However, you will find that you may wish to work with a specific element and elemental for certain work and will want to build an altar for that particular representation accordingly.

Many people feel a natural affinity with the Faery World and find it quite difficult to be part of the physical world of busy traffic, pollution, crowds and modern technology. At one faery workshop that I ran a slender young woman arrived who was quiet and shy and said that she didn't know why she had turned up, but just knew she had to be there.

After I had taken the students through a meditation, to commune with the Faery Kingdom, she just burst into tears. She told the group that she had always felt different, as though she didn't belong to this world and only felt happy when she was out in nature. I explained to her that there are many people on this planet who have been faeries in other lifetimes, who have incarnated this time into human form. These brave faeries have volunteered to become human, in this lifetime, to help clean up the planet and to bring us back into commune with nature.

When we are born, we go through a veil of amnesia and therefore forget, on a conscious level, who we really are. Only on a deep cellular level do we know, and that is why many incarnated faeries feel that they are different, without realizing why. They wonder why they get so angry at animals being mistreated, or when plants and crops are poisoned by chemicals and the total disregard for the planet by humans in general.

As soon as the young faerie delegate related to this, it all made perfect sense to her. The relief and the joy of realizing who she really was and why she felt so different, was wonderful to see.

Faery Glamour Meditation

People like to look their best from time to time, and the faeries are no exception. For they too have their own beauty routine, which is full of magical nature tips and tricks that they are only too willing to share with us, if we will but ask.

If you would like to re-connect with the faery within you and bring some faery beauty into your life find a quiet, comfortable spot, preferably next to a plant or somewhere safe in nature.

So allow yourself to relax, close your eyes, take three deep cleansing breaths and when you are ready, say,

'Faeries of beauty please help me to be dazzling and gorgeous for all life to see. Share, if you will, your tips of the trade. Make me shine with perfection, as you are all made.'

Now see yourself sitting in a field, next to a natural blue pool at the magical faery time of dawn. See the first signs of the Sun as it starts to rise slowly into the morning sky. Soak in its nourishing energy as you relax and listen to the birds sing their early morning chorus. As you look over the field you see small shining orbs of light dancing in the distance. As the lights come nearer they grow brighter and larger until you can quite clearly see that they are faeries, beautiful faeries, who exude absolute radiance. These are the faeries of beauty, who have heard your request and have come to assist.

The faeries lead you over to the crystal blue pool and kneel you down at the water's edge. The water is so clear that you easily see a reflection staring back at you - but not one that you were expecting.

The reflection looks similar to you except for a few remarkable differences - your hair is richer, shining and how you've always desired it to be; your face is smooth and glowing; your eyes sparkle like jewels, and your teeth are pearly white. You see a picture of pure health and dazzling beauty that near takes your breath away. But as you look again, you notice that this isn't all - for protruding from your back are the most ethereal, gossamer wings, you sport elegant elfin-like ears and you wear an outfit made up of delicate petals and fine-spun web.

'This is your faery natural self', sing the Fae of Beauty in unison.

'This is how we see you. Now take a closer look.'

As you peer into the pool you notice that not only do you look beautiful, you are shining from within, illumined! You exude confidence, strength, inner power and, of course, beauty.

Golden energy swirls and dances around you. So breathe in and bathe in your own radiance.

The faeries offer you a sip of freshly collected morning dew, from the healing, sunshine energies of a buttercup. As you drink from this golden cup feel the very life force of nature awaken every part of you. As you assimilate with the potent energies you become as one with the gift that Mother Nature bestows upon you - your own natural beauty - that is, and always has been, there.

When you are ready thank the Beauty Faeries for revealing to you the truth of your perfection. Now take a deep breath and open your eyes, Beautiful One.

Chapter 3

The Magic of Earth

In magical terms the element of Earth is in the direction of the North - the time of Midnight, and the season of Winter; a time when nature goes deep within itself to rest and recharge. The Earth nurtures and restores all that reside in her, as she brings about her gifts that are steeped in magic and mystery.

It is from this rich element that plants, flowers and trees grow and is the very foundations of where we walk, stand and reside, along with the elementals of the Earth.

Earth is home to human-kind and also houses, not only the Gnomes, who are guardians of this element, but also many members of the Elemental Realm, including dwarves who nurture and tend to the crystals and rocks, flower faeries who look like their flower counterparts, dryads of the trees, pixies, elves, fawns, leprechauns, amongst others.

These are the spirits of the Earth that tend to the plants and rocks that grow from and on it and exist in a parallel land to man, in the magical dimension of Faery Land.

The Earth is fertile and stable and is associated with the Goddess, of birth, life, death and re-birth. Earth is the magic of spells from the use of crystals and herbs. In times gone by fertility spells would be made from using acorns and pine cones, in the shape of a wreath and from leaves and flowers. The Earth is nurturing and stable, solid and firm, full of endurance and strength.

Those born under the Earth signs of Capricorn, Taurus and Virgo are considered to be level headed, logical and the most grounded of all the signs. Not surprisingly so! These are the grafters, the hard working ones who see a goal and will not stop until they have reached it, and beyond. Their strength and endurance is to be admired, but they might be wise to take a leaf out of the Air sign's book and rest just once in a while, to allow the creative juices to naturally flow.

Those who have an affinity with the element of Earth love to get their hands dirty, especially in the form of gardening. Growing specific flowers such as Buddleia attracts butterflies and faeries alike. Allowing wild flowers to grow in your garden, such as Foxgloves and Bluebells, works in much the same way.

Never use chemicals to help grow your plants, instead call upon the nature spirits of Earth to assist you and you will find that your flowers bloom beautifully, as well as naturally. You may wish to make yourself a small herb garden, or grow some in a window box.

Choose well for you may wish to incorporate some in spell casting or to make natural flower essences, turning your kitchen into a sacred and magical space.

The dryads are the spirits of the trees and should be respected. These are the wisdom keepers, and hold great knowledge. When I see stumps from roughly hacked fallen trees I send healing light to the dryad who had just lost his home and his *raison d'être*.

The elves are the beings who help and nurture roots of trees and plants and can often be spotted playing within the trees themselves. Elves, like many Earth elementals, are accused of being mischief makers. This is understandable as these are the spirits that make nature tick, and after all nature can be very unpredictable.

The element of Earth is associated with the home and its energy can be used for security, to assist with finances. The Earth faeries love to assist us in the affairs of prosperity and abundance, which is usually brought about in exchange for something we can do for them. Their gifts can often come in quite unexpected ways.

A couple of years ago I met with my lovely friend Debbie, who herself is such a faery in her mannerisms and looks. With her long brown hair, petite frame, pretty features and flowing skirts she looks as though she has just stepped from the pages of a fairy tale. Quiet, thoughtful and softly spoken Debbie has great compassion for the Elemental Realm and on the day we met for a cuppa and a chat she was excited to tell me about an environmental 'clean-up' project she had organised for her co-workers to volunteer for, at the pharmaceutical office she loathed working in.

Debbie had initially been met with resistance but was pleased to report that most had signed up due to her perseverance. As she reached into her new shiny handbag to show me the details she looked surprised and pulled out her hand. As she loosened her grip a beautiful ruby earring was revealed. She gasped, this was part of a pair she had lost two years ago.

She had searched high and low, and felt great loss for them. So how could this earring have been in a bag that had only been bought the previous week? Still reeling from her find she slipped her hand back into the bag and lo and behold retrieved the other ruby earring to complete the pair. Exhilarated we just knew that the Earth faeries had returned her favourite earrings in return for her help.

Sometimes the elementals like to play tricks on us by hiding our personal items. If you would like assistance in finding or retrieving anything lost you can call upon the Earth elementals to assist you.

Earth Magic Finding Spell

Light a brown or black candle and face the direction of North. Take a piece of paper and write upon it the name of that you are looking for. Hold the image of the item in your mind as you say the following incantation...

'Fae of Abundance, guardian of flowers, honour me with your magical powers. Adorn me with riches and the chance to succeed, by

the powers of your Earth energy. There's something I'm missing I just cannot find and picture the item within my clear mind. To find and retrieve from the picture you see, I ask you to return it for safe keeping to me. I work with your magic with harm to none, so mote it be, and it is done'

Blow out the candle and take the piece of paper, folding it four ways, and bury it into the Earth. Your lost item will be returned in an unexpected and magical way.

If you feel drawn to help the Guardians of Earth there are many spells that you can use. Always start by lighting a brown or black candle whilst facing the direction of North. To help the Gnomes visualise soil in the Earth, free of pesticides and chemicals. See it as rich and nourished, and growing from it blooms of flowers, plants, and trees in healthy abundance. Remember that whatever you feel is right to visualise then please do so. The Gnomes are grateful for any assistance and remember whatever you imagine it is done in the Etheric World immediately. With more focus it eventually becomes manifest in our physical dimension. So do keep up the good work.

If you don't already, then look into recycling at home and at work. Encourage others to do the same. Grow your own vegetables and salads if you can, or buy organic. Look out for the wild animals of the Earth by putting food out them. Build shelters for hedgehogs and make sure that the environment around you is 'elemental' friendly.

Working with the Spirits of the Earth

To attune to the beings of Earth spend more time out in the woods and meadows, always asking for permission to enter first, out of respect for the magical beings that live there. Look to see where the spirits of the Earth may like your assistance.

My favourite place to visit is a beautiful lake that is sheltered by woodland on one side and has vast meadows around the rest of its perimeter. The whole area is teeming with wildlife, as well as housing a huge community of Gnomes. I often visit this place to connect with nature and attune with the elementals that reside there. I always turn up with big bags to pick up any garbage that is regrettably dropped by picnickers.

A few years ago I was horrified to discover that the local council had made plans to build a huge waste disposal site just a few hundred metres to the left of the lake. This meant possible noise pollution, hundreds of daily visitors to the site and the general unpleasant energy that goes with it. Not nice for nature or for the Earth elementals that lived in the sacred sanctuary nearby.

Devastated I went as quickly as I could to share the plight with the Gnomes who were fairly cheesed off, to say the least. I asked what I could do to help. With the advice of a few dwarves, they asked me to build a crystal grid to keep the energies of the 'rubbish dump', as we call it in the UK, away. The crystal grid, the dwarves' instructed, would act as a barrier and energy shield thus keeping the chaos out, and the peace of the lake, in. I enlisted the help of my good friend and crystal elemental lover, Donna, who was happy to help.

The crystals were carefully selected we arrived at the lake to set about laying out the grid. This had been shown to me in my mind already, but where to start? We looked around and both saw, at the same time, two sticks on the ground that were laid out like a pointing arrow. We both laughed at how wonderful nature is as we set the first crystal down.

Now, crystals are amazing beings of Spirit, who are guarded and nurtured by dwarves. Each crystal is packed with healing energy of one kind or another and easily attuned, with intention, as they are great memory holders. These guys knew exactly what they were here to do, and we laid them according to the plan that the dwarves had projected into my mind's eye. We left the Gnomes and the dwarves in peace and headed back to my home.

When we arrived we noticed a package on the door step. What could it be? I couldn't believe my eyes when I opened it, for staring at me was a brand new deck of oracle cards by Doreen Virtue, that had just been launched through Hay House publishing called 'Magical Messages from the Fairies'. I explained to Donna that I had not even realised that these cards were available yet, and had not ordered them for that very reason. We laughed with joy and amazement at the powerful manifestation abilities of the Earth elements, and how generous they are when one works in harmony with them.

Yule

Magically speaking Earth is the season of Winter celebrating the festival of Yule. This is a time honoured tradition when our ancestors and faeries alike would gather to welcome the return of the Sun. At Winter Solstice, (usually 21-22 December in the Northern Hemisphere and 21-22 June in the Southern Hemisphere), the Sun appears at its weakest, having waned in strength since the Summer Solstice 6 months earlier. Great cheers ring out in celebration, for the very next Winter's morning the Sun starts its ascent as it becomes stronger as it heads towards the Summer months again.

The new king is heralded, which Celtic tradition honours through tales and legends of a great battle that plays out twice a year between the mighty Holly king and the majestic Oak King. At Summer Solstice the Holly King wins and stands proud through to Winter, until at Yule he is cut down in his prime when Oak King wins and presides over the coming months through until their next battle in Summer.

'Faery folk tip toe soft, across the land of snow and frost, towards a holly tree at Yule, tis time to cut it from its rule. For in this battle, Oak King wins, to lord over months to take through Spring. And in the morn turn to the Sun, who is born again, the light has won! Each

year the sacred wheel doth turn, now Yuletide's here, tis our concern, to celebrate with joy and mirth, may bells ring out for 'peace on Earth'. So place the logs upon the fire, and make wishes of hearts' desire. Honour the flames that warm the cool, with blessings to one and all this Yule.'

Earth Magic Meditation

Breathing deeply with eyes closed you find yourself in Winter. The landscape is covered with snow. It is so beautiful and you breathe in the cold crisp air. You look over to a barren field, the soil ridged from the plough, but now hard and sprinkled with snow. Tall naked trees surround three sides of the field, protecting and stark.

At the far end of the field is a grassy mound and here stands alone a huge ancient oak tree, dominating the sky and its surroundings, branches outstretched welcoming. You stand next to this wise old tree and notice a large door in its trunk. Fearlessly you knock and open the door easily. Inside it is dark and smells of fresh wood.

You enter and find yourself walking down steps that wind round and down, and round and down - at the bottom you notice huge strong roots going further into the earth. It's surprisingly light down here and you can see all sorts of activity. Gnomes and elves beavering away, collecting soil here and taking it there, nurturing the roots of plants that are evenly spaced and lie under the surface of the ground, below the field. Suddenly you realise they are preparing for Spring.

You notice that the energy down here is very strong and rich, and rather intense for you, but you breathe in and feel a rush of Earth magic surge through you. Breathe it in and feel your body pulse with the intensity - very powerful and awakening. You turn to go back up to the door and realise what is providing the light down here, tiny happy glow worms! You delight in how nature provides for itself. You climb back up the winding wooden steps and once back at the grassy knoll you look across the field and the wintery scene.

The sharp, frosty air near takes your breath away. A large beautiful ball of shimmering light appears in front of you. Shining so brightly that you cannot make out the figure inside. A gentle, but authoritative voice of Fae speaks and asks you to hold out your hands.

As you do seven magic beans drop into them. The beans glow like neon lights, and each is a different colour; red, orange, yellow, green, blue, indigo and purple. You sit on a thick rug, which has appeared on the snow-sprinkled grass, under the oak tree as the light-being, of the faery kind, looks on with protecting and healing intention and tells you to make a wish into each bean. As you make a wish into each fluorescent bean, comforting warmth fills and surrounds you.

When you have infused the last bean with a wish you realise that a perfect rainbow streams through you from the base of your spine to the crown of your head. Breathe in the colours, feel the energy and the magic of the wishes that you have just made.

The rainbow expands from you to the other side of the field and you find yourself travelling through the rainbow, through the colours, and as you do so the beans fall to the ground landing in the soil of the barren, snow-sprinkled field.

At the end of the rainbow stands a crock of gold and three leprechauns surround and protect it. The leprechauns greet you, when you arrive, and invite you to look into the huge pot that shines. The gold is so bright that you can't help but breathe up its energy and as you do it fills your body entirely and then bursts up and out of the top of your head, spilling all around you and showering you in gold coins and the energy of abundance and prosperity. Feel that energy, feel the richness - feel the abundance and prosperity surging through you and surrounding you. This energy is now part of you.

You thank the leprechauns and then look across the field. In the distance you can see seven small seedlings, spaced out evenly, all in a row, in the soil. Seven seedlings that are different colours - there's red, orange, yellow, green, blue, indigo and purple. You gasp.

Yes, these are your wishes that were infused in the magic beans, now planted and growing... bringing your dreams to fruition.

Chapter 4

The Magic of Air

In magical terms Air is in the direction of the East - the time of Dawn, and the season of Spring bringing about freedom and new beginnings. The magic of Air stimulates the power of the mind, enhances the intellect and brings about mental clarity.

The Sylphs, who are the Guardians of Air, are the most easy to connect with. We do this naturally as we breathe in the air that is all around us. The Sylphs are flying faeries in form and can be seen, by some with their physical sight, as tiny little pin-pricks of light in the skies, all dancing and swirling in the air.

They work through the gases and ethers of the Earth and are kindly toward humans, especially those who are drawn to use communication, creativity or the performing arts as part of their life purpose. These people have a great affinity with the Sylphs, who are the keepers of inspiration and creativity. They are the ones who bring us aspiration and ideas and assist us in journeying through meditation and connecting with the astral world.

The Sylphs will awaken any mental aspect and, when asked, assist with creative writing, poetry and even exams. These spirits of Air are the magical beings who fuel our imagination and encourage us to make wishes and dream big. But they won't let us stop there for they urge us take action in pursuing our goals and can help bring about success. They are the ones who make sure that the right doors open at the right time and put in place the people who can help make our dreams happen.

Those who are born under the Air signs of Aquarius, Gemini and Libra are naturally creative. These are the poets, the writers, the performers and dreamers. Air signs have often been accused of sitting around day dreaming instead of facing reality and if they could they would rather stick their nose in a good novel than be out there grafting.

Those born under the Earth signs could teach Air signs a thing or two about that, and the Earth elementals would be helpful in assisting Air signs to become a little more grounded too.

Having an affinity with the element of Air means you love to be out in nature, to be one with the breeze. This element has the highest vibratory rate, which is why one always feels better from a brisk walk, a blow by the sea or by simply sitting outside.

Breathing in the air is nourishment for the body and refreshment for the spirit. It can be used, on an etheric level, to 'blow away the cobwebs', meaning that it eliminates and removes any negative aspects that may be very weighing on one's mind.

Like the winds, Sylphs can be volatile and changeable. The winds are their vehicle, from each of the four directions...

- **North Wind** - Named Boreas, of Winter, who is icy cold, and brings the sleet and snow.
- **East Wind** - Named Eurus, who is fresh and brings light Spring rains.
- **South Wind** - Named Notus, who is warm and gentle, bringer of a Summer breeze.
- **West Wind** - Named Zephryus, who brings the harsh beating rains from the West.

In Air magic we can work with these winds and determine the direction we wish the Sylphs to travel in. All you need is a clear intention of which wind you would like to call upon, face that direction and blow. As you do you will feel the change in the wind as the Sylphs change direction.

Play and have fun with the Sylphs, be very aware of the changes and how they feel. This is a great way to become familiar with the way of the winds. Soon you will instinctively recognise any of the winds the moment you step outside. Our ancestors worked in this way and they were always aware of any omens that had been left in their path as a message from the world of the Fae.

The Sylphs also call us to do their bidding, but often leave us a gift in return. My attention had caught a piece of paper that was flying in the breeze, one afternoon. I was rather concerned as I do not like trash to litter up the countryside and so I went to retrieve it. As I reached to grab it from the ground the wind picked up and lifted the paper from me.

This game of chase continued for quite a while, and I was quite aware of the Sylphs teasing me each time they snatched the paper away, until it finally landed in its resting place. As I snatched the piece of paper it revealed a shiny jewelled bracelet that was lying underneath it, on the grass. The Sylphs brought me to a great reward indeed.

Not only do the Sylphs bring us their messages on the whisper of a breeze, they often bring us signs through the formations of clouds and gift us with the drop of a feather.

Air Magic Spell

Collect four feathers from nature (that have fallen in front of you or that you have found in your path).

Name the first feather, Boreas. If there is a situation you would like to banish from your life put your intentions for it to be frozen out of your life, upon the winds of the North. Name the second feather, Eurus. If you would like to bring about new beginnings, to travel, for clarity of mind, creativity, inspiration, then put your wishes and intentions into this feather of the East.

Name the third feather, Notus. To bring love, passion, romance or to overcome heartbreak put your wishes and intentions into this feather of the South. Name the fourth feather, Zephyrus. To help heal emotions, for cleansing, for dreamwork or enhancing psychic abilities focus your wishes into this feather of the West.

Now, standing outside in nature, face North and throw the first feather in that direction, allowing the winds of Boreas to take it. Throw the second feather to the East, into the winds of Eurus. Face the South and throw the third feather into the Winds of Notus. Throw the fourth feather as you face the direction of West, into the winds of Zephyrus.

If the winds of a particular direction are not strong, and have not carried your feather into the direction you have intended then observe where each feather has landed. Take note of any meaning that might come to you, for this is your first steps of Faery Wind Divination.

Thank the Sylphs for assisting in bringing about your wishes, as you respect their flexibility.

Working with the Spirits of the Air

If you want to bring about the gifts that the Sylphs have to offer then you should invoke them and incorporate the element of Air into your world. Connect with them by taking long walks in the hills and feel the Sylphs as they blow through your hair. Talk to the Sylphs as you connect with the breeze, and listen to their answers that come to you through your thoughts or in signs that they send to acknowledge your connection with them - as they did me one brisk Winter's morning:

I visited my favourite nature spot on a very sunny but cold, crisp day. There wasn't a cloud in the sky and I sat by the frozen lake surrounded by tall stark trees, on a rather frosty wooden bench.

As I basked in the warmth of the Winter's sun I closed my eyes and focussed on my breathing. I recognised that the breeze was coming in an easterly direction and so I opened my heart chakra to the Sylphs. In my mind's eye I saw the faeries of the Air receiving the love that I was sending out on my exhale. As I inhaled deeply I imagined breathing their love back to me, filling my heart. And so it continued for quite a while as I breathed my love out to the Sylphs, and breathed their love back to me in return.

When I felt ready to open my eyes, I looked up. A small light aircraft suddenly appeared and seemed to be doing acrobatics in the sky directly above me. Within seconds it completely vanished, but left behind a huge white fluffy HEART shape, which stood out boldly against the blue of the winter's sky.

I gasped as I realised that this was a sign in response to the connection that had just been experienced. The Sylphs had sent me a sign to acknowledge that the love felt was very real. I knew instantly in that moment with their love and support, anything is possible.

We can connect with the Sylphs through the sounds of wind chimes or instruments, such as the flute which are all associated with the element of Air. Give back to the Sylphs by feeding the birds during the cold months, visualise the air clear of pollution and light a yellow candle to bring about your healing intention.

Introduce music, dance and song into your life and as the Sylphs draw to you you will find that you become healed in many ways, opening up a new world of creativity, opportunity and inspiration.

Beltane

Magically speaking Air is the season of Spring when it celebrates the magical Festival of Beltane, usually April 31st - May 1st. This is the one aged old Pagan celebration that has not been 'Christianised', and today in the United Kingdom, and beyond, it is still honoured.

Villagers gather to eat together and sup ale as they are treated to traditional Morris dancing and a May Queen is chosen. Local children weave ribbons in and out as they dance around a decorated May-pole. This is a phallic symbol representing the traditional rituals that were once held to promote fertility for livestock and people alike.

Great Bel fires were lit on hills as a sign of protection and others were lit for couples to leap over hand in hand before running into the woods to consummate their union. This is a time of the blending of energies of the feminine and masculine, to celebrate the sacredness of sexuality. The Goddess takes on the God as her lover, in order to give birth to the full bloom of nature during summer months to come.

Beltane marks the return of full life and nature is fully honoured in the fresh bright flowers, grasses and leaves that have started to push through. Beltane is a time of embracing and honouring the new creative power that is stirring in the world of nature.

'With fires lit across the land, a couple leaps whilst hand in hand, to mark their union and this rite, for they know tonight's the night! As they run into the darkened wood, and find a grassy glade they should, remember well of who's around, for bands of faeries all surround, the couple as they consummate, the faeries cheer and seal the fate, of plants and flowers, shrubs and trees, whilst the God's upon his knees, impregnating the mother to be, from sowing deep his natural seed. And so in time the Goddess will birth, the magic that's nature, on this Earth.'

Healing Faery Meditation

Whenever you are feeling under the weather, depressed, lacking energy or inflicted with pain, you can call upon the faeries of the Air to help you heal. These faeries are natural healers and know how to instantly bring about relief and cure to your dis-ease.

All you need to do is lie in a comfortable position, preferably at night-time so that these healing faeries can continue to work with you as you sleep. Don't forget to thank the faeries whole-heartedly, when you awake and leave them a small plate of bread and honey as grateful payment.

So feeling relaxed, take a deep breath in and slowly release, breathe in and out, another deep breath in, and release. See yourself fully protected and safe as your guardian angel watches over you and say aloud or in your mind…

'Faeries of Air come heal my pain, with your powerful magic, I ask not in vain. Bring me cures from new cobwebs and bright starlight made, and let the discomfort and illness now fade.'

With eyes still shut see, in your mind, a bright shining light above your head, glistening and twinkling like a beautiful silver star against the backdrop of a black velvet night sky. Watch as this star becomes bigger and brighter, expanding above you until it bursts - and thousands and thousands of silver and pearl beads of light explode into the air. As you look carefully, you see that these aren't beads at all, they are tiny beings of light, full of energy, swirling around you.

In the centre of each light being glows an ember of the brightest blue - these are the healing faeries. As you take a deep breath in, these remarkable healers come together and form an iridescent blanket of sparkling silver and sapphire, like a giant spider's web glistening on a bright frosty morning. This magical jewelled cloak wraps around your body causing a surge of warm healing energy to pulse through you, filling every vessel, every artery, every part of your very being.

You are filled with perfect love, healing and strength as the faeries touch your soul and your heart with their magic. Breathe in the healing energy - feel it. Breathe in the healing light - experience it. Stay in the moment - rest and allow, as vitality and wholeness are restored.

Chapter 5

The Magic of Fire

In magical terms Fire is in the direction of the South, it is the time of Noon, and the season of Summer. The magic of Fire brings about lust, passion, attraction, illumination, love, sex, sun, warmth and inner power!

Out of all the element guardians the Salamanders are probably the least known, but every time we boil the kettle, switch on a light or use the oven we are communing with them.

Our ancestors connected well with these magical beings, as they gathered together around fires to share stories of their day as well as ones of myth and legend. Offerings of incense or herbs would be sprinkled into the fire to honour and thank the spirits who were working hard to keep the fiery furnace alive.

It is so sad that today most people do not realise that the nature beings and elements contribute to the workings of this world. How many women for instance thank the Salamanders for assisting in blow drying or straightening their hair each morning? But magical people have a deep affinity with Salamanders as they recognise these 'elemental beings' within the flames of the candles they use for spell work.

A lit flame can be seen from the Spirit World. It is the only physical connection that can be seen from one realm to the other, which is why we light a candle for those who have passed over. Next time you do, know that your deceased loved one can actually see it!

What I find absolutely amazing about fire is that it cannot be felt or seen or even exist in this world without us physically creating it. We cannot do this without the help, the ignition and spark of the Salamanders. Sometimes you may wonder why a fire will not take, or a match will not burn.

Perhaps you have not asked and gently coaxed the guardian of Fire to be willing and present. It is a very sensible thing to honour and appease these Keepers of Flames.

If you wish for them to appear, or if you would like to be kept safe from the ravishing effects that fire can sometimes create then please give the Salamanders the respect they deserve. They are the ones who control the fire after all. Give them thanks, or a small gift in appreciation for bringing about light and warmth into this physical realm.

Other Fire elementals include the smaller Fire sprites and Fire faeries who are the drive behind attraction and desire. They too can be called upon to work on awakening the spiritual kundalini energy that often lies dormant within each one of us. The djinn are Arabian desert faeries that are even mentioned in the Qur'an, indicating that they are nature spirits made of a smokeless and 'scorching fire'. They have the power to travel great distances at record speed, just as one would expect a ravaging fire to spread.

Salamanders are bringers of strength, of courage. They are the motivating force that assists us in igniting our inner flame of passion, fuelling us to be able to walk in our true light and seize our life time's purpose, with full might, vitality and vigour.

Those who are born under the Fire signs of Aries, Leo and Sagittarius are often accused of being hot-headed. But these are the people with great drive and confidence as the Salamanders are great allies in assisting to bring about all you need to succeed.

Fire signs may, however, benefit from working with more of the sensitive elementals, of Water for instance. They may find that they need to look at a situation from another's point of view or to empathise with someone else's feelings. Elementals will always come to you when you are ready to work with them.

Being Libran, an Air sign, I have always looked at fairness and justice and like everything in harmony. However, I lacked the drive that the elementals desired me to have, in order to be their 'voice'. A year after I began to take my faery workshops nationwide I felt an overwhelming desire to colour my beautiful long, blonde hair bright red!

This was something I jumped into, assuring myself I would not regret. I didn't until the day I found out that I could not reverse the process and would now remain, what looked like, a fiery red-head.

That night I slept deeply and in the dreamtime was surprised to find a bright red and orange Salamander looking up at me as he lay heavily on my Solar Plexus chakra, in my midriff. I did not want him there and asked him to move. He would not budge! I screamed out for my soul sister, Barbara, to remove him. But she explained that she could not, for he had work to do.

The next morning, feeling a little perturbed, I attended a faery fayre, where I was giving a talk. At the fayre a gentleman approached me and handed me a gift, telling me that he didn't know what the significance was or why he was giving this to me. I opened the little jewelled box and pulled out a silver chain with a pendant of a coloured Salamander dangling from it. Okay, I got the message, good and proper.

The following year I met with Native American Lakota teacher, Ed McGaa, Eagle Man, who gifted me my Spirit Name of 'Red Spirit Woman' as we worked together within the hot Salamander energy of a sweat lodge. The Salamanders have ignited my path of destiny from within, giving me the strength and passion to continue my work, and theirs.

Fire Magic Salamander Spell

To invoke Salamander energy find a quiet place to sit, facing South, and light a red candle. Gazing into the flame say...

'Salamanders, Spirits of Fire, bring me your courage and all I desire. Ignite the flame of passion within, so I can connect with the strength of the Djinn. With honour, respect, I call upon you- please help me to work my life purpose through. Extinguish the dark that

blacks out the light, so I am released of fears and my plight. Allow the fire to ravage me, to purify, cleanse and set me free. I am of power, this I know, as I become the sacred glow. Dear beings of light, of Summer and Sun, with my heart I give thanks, there, it is done.'

Feel yourself getting warmer as you watch the flame expand and become embraced within the vivid colours of red, gold and orange. Connect with the power and the life-giving force of Fire whilst breathing in the energy of the Salamanders, as their essence fills your entire body, awakening every cell.

Allow the re-calibration as you attune to the high Salamander frequency, thus enabling you to connect with the energy and attributes that these beings have to offer. When you feel that this is completed, blow out the candle. Let the swirl of the extinguished flame wrap around you and say...

'Gratefully I accept the magic of you, of protection to assist in all that I do. Lend me the courage, build power in me, and assist my transcendence, So Mote It Be.'

Give thanks to the Salamanders knowing that whenever you connect with the fire of the Sun, when you light a flame, use an electrical appliance and of course when in meditation your magical fiery relationship is invoked and the fire within, stoked.

Working with the Spirits of Fire

The magic of Fire is also greatly present within live volcanoes. As I write this I am sitting in the Sorrento hills of Italy, looking out at the great Mount Vesuvius. It is best known for its eruption in AD 79 that led to the burying and destruction of the Roman cities of Pompeii and Herculaneum, and is still very much alive today.

Since I was a child it has called me and now being within its very presence condemns me to feeling a great fearful respect, knowing that it could erupt at any given time, knowing that it has taken thousands of lives. It is surprising though how many people live at the foot this mountain, despite offerings of relocation of families and businesses alike by the Italian government.

I completely understand why they do not wish to move for Mount Vesuvius feels alive. Within its very structure Salamanders dance and bubble, urging to leap and escape the shell and fly through the skies and cover the Earth. I wonder how many of these inhabitants, who are reluctant to leave, actually make offerings to the spirit of this mighty volcano. How many honour and revere the element and elementals of Fire that are housed within it?

Lightning is a flash of Salamander physical manifestation. We are warned to stay away, to keep indoors, for fear of getting struck by it. Lightning is something that has always excited me.

Barbara was struck by lightning at thirteen years old. She was playing in a tree when it struck her on the back of her neck. She felt a power surge through her, recovered immediately, but told no-one. Years later she visited a Native American reservation and during ceremony the Lakota Chief gave her a knowing nod as he silently handed her a 'Lightning Stick'. A great honour indeed!

On hearing this story I wished with all my might to have the same experience, to be struck by Salamanders in their mighty manifestation of lightning. Oh the power! That evening I plugged my cell phone charger into the socket. Bang! It was faulty and I was rushed to A&E having had an electric shock. Fortunately I was fine, but it made complete sense of the phrase 'be careful what you wish for'!

Working with Fire energy, in an etheric sense, is a great healing. Imagining etheric flames purging through any negative energy, raging and consuming any darkness that lies within oneself, which has formed from any negative thoughts and feelings, helps to move one forward and gets rid of what no longer serves.

A sensible faery has just whispered in my ear to be sure to give a health and safety warning about the dangers of playing with fire! I giggled, but am obliged to obey. As I have already advised, early in this chapter, take heed and respect the presence of the Salamander and the element of Fire, and you will be protected.

The Sun is the greatest example of the element of Fire and the impassioned work of the Salamanders. Many ancient cultures worshipped this life-giving entity, such as the Egyptians who saw the Sun as the god, Ra. The Ancient Greeks honoured it as their god 'Helios', the Romans 'Apollo' and the Celts, 'Lugh'. Today many of the remaining Native American Tribes perform a Sun Dance each year to honour the Sun as the bringer of life.

Litha

Magically speaking Fire is the season of Summer, when is celebrated the Sun festival of Litha, or Summer Solstice, which is when the Sun is at its highest point in the sky. This is usually around 21st-22nd June in the Northern Hemisphere, and 21st-22nd December in the Southern Hemisphere, and has been the most significant time of Sun worship since the birth of mankind itself.

Today, I am pleased to say it is still a great time of celebration, honouring and of great spiritual importance for many. Those who are not aware of such connotation still, albeit unwittingly, worship the Sun in other ways. For they partake in outdoor parties, barbecues and topping up their tans during the hot and passionate months of Summer, unaware that the faeries of fire are playing their part.

Midsummer Magic Meditation

Make a 'faery ring - sprinkle a circle of faery dust, dried leaves, grasses, flowers etc. Close your eyes and see, in your mind's eye, this circle come to life - as mushrooms and toadstools spring up, creating a magical circle. Grasses and moss grow in between the fungi and tiny little flowers open up.

Smell the sweet scent of the grass and flowers, mixed with the earthy scent of the mushrooms. Feel, or see, strong roots grow from the soles of your feet down into the ground, stretching deep, deep into the earth and wrapping around a huge crystal - grounding you, protecting you and connecting you to Mother Earth.

Breathe up the earth energy, breathe up the earth magic and feel it fill you. See or feel a beautiful light coming down from the heavens, through the top of your head filling you with angel energy - of protection and love.

Look around the perimeter of the faery ring - notice the energy that has grown around the ring - like a wall of gold that spins around the circle. Creating an energy field that transcends time and space.

Focus on the fairy ring and say,

'I create this ring in honour of the Fae And ask for protection on this Midsummer's Day. As I enter this portal of where the veil is thin I ask that the faeries welcome me, within.'

Hold the intention that this is for the highest good and that no harmful thing comes from your visit. Ask, and listen using your intuition, for where you should be within the circle and step carefully into the ring. Have a look around in your mind's eye - what do you see? What do you feel? What's around you? Notice the faery energy, for today is the strongest time for workings of faery magic. Allow yourself to be part of the Midsummer magic and breathe it in. Feel it surge through you.

This is your opportunity to ask the Fae to help you to make your dreams come true,

'Calling the faeries to colour my dreams. Paint them with moonlight

and golden sunbeams. Fill me with magic I ask of this too. Please grant me my wishes that they may come true.'

Now tell the faeries what you wish for in your life - and be sure to project your desires for the highest good of all. Listen to what the faeries have to say, as they may give you advice or instructions, and allow them to grant your wish in their own unique way for you. Let them perform their ritual for you to experience.

Some faery folk approach with a beautiful goblet which bears the Sun's image. They tell you that this is in honour of the Sun God, of whom they celebrate on this day when its energy is at its peak. They offer you the goblet - it is filled with liquid sunshine. You may take it, and as you sip - courage, integrity, strength, power, righteousness, confidence and higher ability pour into you...

Hand the goblet back and take a moment as these energies you have just consumed are assimilated into your essence... You feel more energised and connected than you have ever done before. You reach into your pocket - you have a gift that you offer as a thank-you to all who have welcomed you and helped you here today in the faery ring.

You hear the words 'Let us take you by the hand and dance with you in Faeryland!' So dance now, move, have fun as the spirits of plants, trees, flowers and stones all participate - until every part of nature has joined the dance. Dance with all your heart in the Midsummer sunlight and allow yourself to be completely free!

When you have finished the dance, bid goodbye to your new friends and step carefully out of the faerie's ring, back into your own world. Bringing with you a new sense of magic and wonder, your life will never be the same again.

Chapter 6

The Magic of Water

In magical terms Water is the time of Dusk, it is the direction of West and is the season of Autumn, where nature starts to turns within itself and we reflect on wherever we have been, what we have done in the preceding months.

The magic of Water helps us to achieve balance, harmony, inner peace, tranquillity and to unwind! When we take a bath or a shower we immediately receive the healing and cleansing benefits of Water, both physically and metaphysically.

The magical Guardians of Water, the Undines, can be asked to assist us with filling up our inner storerooms with an abundance of riches as well as bringing about prophetic dreams, enhancing our psychic abilities and helping to heal our emotions.

Those of you who are born under the Water signs of Pisces, Cancer and Scorpio may have often been accused of being over emotional or too sensitive. The truth is that sensitivity is a beautiful gift. It helps you to feel for others, to be both empathetic and sympathetic.

It also opens your heart so that you are more readily open to hear the voice and messages of the Fae. What you may wish to ask the Undines for, however, is to assist you in being aware of whose feelings are affecting you. Are they yours or those of somebody else? The art is to observe how you are feeling and come to a realisation that you are not your feelings.

Soon you will go into whatever emotion comes up, and discover where it has come from and why. You will find that you will act accordingly and react in a different way, with a more masterful approach.

The Undines come in various forms, such as mer-faeries, water sprites and water nymphs. These are the guardians of smaller bodies of water, such as lakes, pools, streams and rivers, including the plants and animals within the waters.

Selkies are Scottish mermaids who shapeshift from their form as a seal into beautiful women, in order to lure a young man to marry. Often a selkie will leave her husband to return to the ocean. I believe that Hans Anderson's Little Mermaid was really a selkie!

The most famous of all the Undines are the mermaids. These are the guardians of the seas, who nurture and tend to all that is alive and growing within these huge bodies of waters that covers at least two-thirds of our planet.

Since ancient times the ocean has always fascinated mankind. Greek and Roman mythical stories tell of their Gods, Poseidon and Neptune, ruling the waves and of sailors' sightings of beautiful women donning a huge fish tail, instead of legs, appearing within the waters.

Tales abound of shipwrecks caused by the beauty and allurement of sirens who called to seafarers through the heavenly sounds of their seductive songs, and mermaid's diving deeply down, uncovering lost treasures of the deep. Of course we can use these tales as metaphors to represent the searching of our own riches that lie dormant deep within ourselves, just waiting to be discovered.

Mermaids are said to cause destruction and the drowning of sailors and ships, but there are also tales of mermaids rescuing would-be drown victims and taking them safely to shore. These tales represent the unpredictable ways of the oceans, of which of course the mermaids are part of, as the spirits of Water.

There is scientific evidence, through the work of Dr Masaru Emoto that water holds onto memory. Which is why we pray over water, for it will hold onto everything that is imbued into it.

I draw love hearts, ancient power symbols and those of protection on my drinking water bottles and the kettle, ensuring that I consume water that is filled only with love and good intentions.

Likewise, the saints and prophets healed with water infused with their prayers, for they knew of the memory, and therefore the energy, water holds. There are many specific bodies of waters all over the world that are used for healing, such as the Chalice Well in Glastonbury, United Kingdom, the River Jordan and the Miraculous Spring of Our Lady Apparitions Grotto in Lourdes, France.

The energy grows within the water and is built stronger each day by the number of visitors who put their prayers and wishes into it, thus creating an energetic whirlpool of the people's wants and desires.

Wishing wells have the same effect, and are found worldwide. I have recently visited the famous Trevi Fountain in Rome. Above stands a huge baroque confection of thrashing mer-horses, splashing water, and striding tritons presided over by a muscular Neptune, guarding the clear blue waters of the pool itself.

I watched as hundreds of tourists all fought for a position to make their wishes whilst tossing in coins. This is little more than an exchange, one that is made with the water spirits in return for bringing about what the wish-maker desires.

Mermaids are magical beings who can manifest their desires in an instant. All they have to do is visualise what they desire and it is theirs in an instant. This is how they heal and help the water plants and creatures that they are guardian to, to grow fully - by seeing them as 'whole' in their mind's eye, and it is done.

Water Magic Ocean Spell

The mermaids are calling us to help clean up the pollution that has infected not only their world, but also that of all living beings who inhabit the seas and oceans - and of course the water itself. If you are feeling the call and would like to assist, here is a simple, but effective healing spell that the mermaids will receive well.

You will need a bowl of water, sea salt, gold candle, sea shells, crystals, stones, paper and pencil, optional: CD of the sound of waves, seaweed, incense.

Fill the bowl with water and place it in front of you facing West, for West is the direction of the element of Water. Add in a few pinches of natural sea salt and also any crystals, shells or stones to the water. Imagine a bubble of protective light all around you. Now ignite the candle and place it safely in front of you and say...

'Spirits of water, mermaid in me, I offer to help heal all beings of sea, May the waters be cleansed to whole purity, let the clearing begin, so mote it be.'

Now tear the paper into small pieces and write a word of healing on each; words that the ocean would benefit from, such as: clear, whole, pure, healed, revitalised, energised, beauty, purified etc. (The mermaids will direct you here and give you words that they know the oceans need to heal with.)

Now wrap each piece of paper individually around a stone, shell or crystal and submerse them into the water. Now see in your mind's eye the oceans of this planet receiving the healing gifts that those words represent.

Bring your focus to the flame of the candle, and watch golden/orangey light flicker on top of the golden wax. Now, using intention, send a golden light to the water in front of you. See, in your mind's eye the water in front of you receiving this blast of high vibrational healing light and intend this for all the oceans and seas. As this is received the mermaids offer their energy to take this light out to all the waters that cover the land, healing and regenerating all inhabitants and waters across the globe. When you know in your heart that it is done, blow out the candle and say...

*'By the power of water, of ocean and sea. With thanks I return, so
mote it be.'*

Working with Spirits of Water

Charm, allurement, seduction, beguilement - these are the traits
of the mermaid, the witches or Goddesses of the waters.
Mermaids take pride in their appearance and know that their
long flowing tresses represent their untamed sexuality and
magical abilities. Hair is looked upon as extremely powerful and
in times gone by was used as a keepsake or a token of affection
when given to a loved one.

Long hair is the mark of the Fae, particularly red hair and is
often used in spells. Today women, and men, cut their hair
without realising that they are in fact disempowering
themselves. To the Fae cutting their hair short marked grief or
mourning.

Magical practitioners recognise the power of hair and are
careful not to let their own fall into the wrong hands, for
unwanted spell work can be cast upon you unwittingly if it does.
When I comb my hair I always keep any 'fall-out' for the birds,
to help insulate their nests, or to offer to the spirits as an
honouring and a token of my appreciation.

I can remember as a little girl pretending to sit on a rock,
whilst at the local swimming pool, combing my long blonde hair.
I would then fall into the pool and swim with my imaginary
dolphin friends as I dived in and out of the water, allowing my
hair to swirl all around me as I twisted and turned.

Mirror magic is a firm favourite with mermaids, for the glass
itself represents the psychic abilities of water. The mirror is used
as a portal to the astral world. Whilst gazing into a handheld
mirror the mermaid understands the power of reflection. If you
wish to bring something about then find a hand held mirror,

which you may wish to decorate using shells, netting and crystals.

As you stare into the mirror, start to invoke your power by brushing your hair whilst stating positive affirmation, intentions and desires. You may wish to bring about romance, riches or affirm your beauty and so open your mind's eye by seeing all that you wish for in the reflection staring back at you.

Bath time is a relaxing pastime for the would-be mermaid. Remembering that water holds memories, put your wishes, prayers and intentions into the water as it fills the bath. Sprinkle and stir in sea salts, which will help you to relax whilst you soak, as well as revive your spirit. Placing sea shells and crystals of blue, green and turquoise around the tub will help you connect with the energies of the sea and I often like to add a few lit candles to the ambience.

Swimming is another must for many and I know of mermaid enthusiasts who long to, or actually do, live near the ocean - or at least have a pond in their backyard! Interestingly there are quite a few mermaid fans who can't actually swim. However, I can remember on insisting on swimming without aids at just four years old, and naturally swam with ease under the water. I just couldn't resist!

Many healers recognise the benefits of working with crystals, but do not underestimate the healing properties of sea shells. Remember that shells are a direct connection with the animals of the ocean and the sea itself. They have been imbued with the cleansing salt of the ocean as well the strength of sunlight and the magical effects of the Moon and the stars.

Samhain

Magically speaking Water is the season of Autumn which celebrates the Celtic festival of Samhain, or Halloween as it is more commonly known, October 31st - November 1st.

Today Samhain conjures up ghosts, pumpkin lanterns and

children shouting 'Trick or Treat!', as they hungrily hold out bags for candy. Traditionally though this was an old Celtic celebration of Summer's end.

Fires were lit on the night of 31st October and villagers would burn crops and animals to their Gods and Goddesses to share with them, and to give thanks for the bounty of the harvest. The Celts believed that the souls of the dead of the Underworld were set free for that night, of which some were welcomed and others feared.

Costumes and masks worn were for protection from these spirits. Samhain today is still considered a time of connection and reflection on those who have left this world for the other, and to look at where we ourselves have journeyed from and to, during the wheel of the year.

The Goddess has become the Crone and we are invited to draw on her wisdom from deep within as she cradles us during the dark months to come, as we release all that no longer serves us.

The veil between the worlds is at its thinnest and a good time to see and connect with the Faery World. It is said, however, that they are more malevolent beings at this time of year and an old custom was to hang dried apples above one's doorway as a mark of protection from any mischief.

'Cauldrons boiling, lanterns are shining, ghouls, ghosts, groans are whining. Parties sweep across the land. Children, adults, hand in hand. Time of fun but must remember, as fires burn bright and glow with embers, our ancestors who walked before. We honour thee and ask for more, wisdom, tools, to help us be, the wise amongst us, let us see, through veil, whilst thin, this very night, protection in place, no need for fright. So we welcome you and all you bring, go deep inside and look within, to shed the old, a shamanic death, embraced and warmed within the Earth, inviting in life anew, the Goddess calls for it to be you, Through the year from Maiden to Mother, the

end is now, to feel the other. In her glory stands the Crone. Don't be afraid to stand alone. This sacred path leads you to be free. Go forth in strength, so mote it be.'

Mermaid Magic Meditation

To connect with the magic of the mermaids we need to raise our energies to their vibration. We can do this through visualisation meditation, an easy way to access different dimensions. Once we have connected with our inner mermaid, we are more able to harness our natural powerful manifestation abilities and reap the magic and abundance that has been bubbling under the surface.

So you are invited to dive in and stir the siren within you, to uncover your own hidden treasure that is waiting to be revealed.

Inhale the sea air. Become one with the waves - breathe in, breathe out, breathe in, breathe out. Feel the ocean - you are part of it. Breathe in those waves; inhale the surf into your very being. Feel the release as the waves crash against the shore. Breathe in and exhale as the tide pulls back again. You are standing on the shore, watching the ocean - watching the foam as it slides up the beach, and then back again into the waters. Look across the water - see the shimmering light dancing on the surface, as the sun beams down upon it.

Feel that familiarity, feel that wanting, that needing, that absolute urge - you have to be a part of the ocean, you are a part of it and your yearning is like never before.

Walk slowly down to the edge of the sea - let the waves gently lap your feet. Look down and see the sand amongst your toes and step further forwards into the water, washing away the sand.

Feel the coolness - your body gets used to it quickly - and wade forward, through the water, further and further out until you realise you are floating and you stretch out your arms and turn onto your back. You look toward your feet, floating horizontally in front of you - but instead of your feet, you see a large, beautiful fish tail - all the way down from your hips.

With a gasp, you recognise it immediately and move so that you can touch it with your hands, feel it, splash about with it.

See the colour, see how it shimmers - dive in and out of the water. Do you remember the weight of it? And yet it is easy to move and you feel so powerful.

Dive down into the water - swimming deeper and deeper, through the cool clear waters - so refreshing - deeper and deeper - feeling more and more at ease with your surroundings, more familiar - relaxed. Further and further and deeper, down to the depths of the ocean. Feel your heart skip a beat as you come across some ancient ruins at the sea bed. Pillars, an arch - you swim through. Oh my, you recognise this place, filled with crumbling buildings, once glorious and now ancient. Have a good look around, swim in and out of pillars, over walls, around old mosaic floors.

You then come across a doorway and you enter into a dark cave - swim, swim - keep going until you see a glimpse of light.

As the light gets brighter you find yourself in the most glorious seabed room, decorated with the jewels of the sea - sparkling and shimmering in the sunlight that filters down from the top of the ocean through an open hole in what was once a ceiling. You know this room - have a look around. Now you remember, this is your room - the room where you received all those gifts, the abundance, the treasure - all part of your birthright. Take a moment and think back to then. Poseidon, Neptune - feel their energies, the energies of your family, from whence you are really from.

You look down and see a trap door - yes, this is it. Pull the handle, it releases the door easily - and as you look down a huge, trunk floats up toward you and you grab it and put it to one side on the seabed. Kneeling in front of it you turn the key of the small lock at the front of the chest and open the lid. You gasp - and then squint your eyes - the bright light that emanates from the chest is quite blinding. Focusing your eyes, you now know why - the chest is crammed with treasures - gold, diamonds, rubies and emeralds, tiaras, necklaces, bracelets and rings. Have a look through - go on - seem familiar? This is your treasure. This treasure is your birth-right. This treasure is and has always been yours. This treasure always will be.

Tucked carefully underneath the lid is a golden envelope - with your name on it. Carefully open the envelope - it is from the great Sea King himself, Neptune – your father. It tells you of what is yours and how it always has been - but most of all, it tells you of how you can access it right now and forever.

Read the note - it is for you after all.

After you've read the note, you put it back into the golden envelope and tuck it back in its place, under the lid. Move the chest to the entrance of the trap-door and see it lower gently in the water. This is your place and you can come back at any time to read your letter and access your treasure at any time. In fact, all you have to do is see the chest in your mind's eye and absolutely know that all the treasures it contains comes easily to you - there is no way that it cannot, for it is your birth-right - it fills your bank account, your purse and anywhere that you desire it to be.

You feel a new surge of energy sweep up through your tail, up through your body, your face and out of the crown of your head, surrounding you entirely - it's electric - it is the magical energy of abundance. The Universe can only respond in one way now - and that is to match what you now have.

Feeling and knowing that you surrounded with riches, take a deep breath and swim out of the ancient ruins - through the pillared entrance and swim up - and up and up. Through the cool clear waters, feeling refreshed, feeling alive and so abundant!

With a mighty push you come to the surface and gasp as you feel the warm Sun on your face. As you swim around you feel so liberated, so free with no restrictions - feel your long flowing hair, following your movements as you as you twist and turn. Look at the colour of your hair - isn't it beautiful? So soft and shiny.

You look down and notice something that is a beautiful orange with dusty pink and you dive down to take a closer look. It is a comb, made of coral. You retrieve it and with a mighty push you swim upwards, to the surface. With a gasp, you feel the warm sun on your face and swim across to a smooth rock that is jutting up out of the sea. With ease you hoist yourself up and make yourself comfortable on the rock. You pull your long, long hair round to your left side and start to pull the coral comb through it. Even though it is very tangled from the mixture of sea salt and the drying on the sun, you realise that you have missed this activity. You continue to try and comb your hair whilst basking in the golden warm light, and you hum a simple tune.

After a while, you decide that the tangles won't come out completely and you dive back into the sea - immediately your hair returns back to being soft and silky, waving around as you move.

You continue to enjoy the freedom of floating around you - and then begin to sense something very familiar, something is coming, something that you are very connected with. You swim upwards toward the surface again and suddenly feel an object come beneath you and you are tossed high into the air and land back into the water - SPLASH!

With a gasp you look around to see what had caused such a thing and you see a long, sleek grey nose practically touching yours, you pull back a bit and immediately recognise those dancing eyes - yes, it's your dolphin. Your play-mate and best friend. With a squeal of joy your fling your arms around him. He nods for you to get on to his back, and although he is slippery, your tail grips magnificently.

Away you go - oh what fun, as your dolphin glides through the water you breathe in the salty air, the colours, the surroundings and the spray. This is heaven, this is who you are. After a while the dolphin starts to swim towards the shore. Oh, but you don't want to go back, you want to stay. You jump off your friend and put your hand gently on his nose as you look deep into his eyes. His eyes are deep and penetrating - full of wisdom.

Yes, you know what he is communicating to you. You must go back to human form, you agreed a long time ago to fulfil a mission that was much needed. The dolphin assures you that your efforts aren't in vain and are much appreciated.

He also reminds you that you can come back at any time and that his magic, and all of the magic of the ocean, is with you at all times - supporting you. The secret, he winks, is to remember exactly who you really are. You sigh, a sigh of blissful awareness - and in a blink the dolphin is gone.

You step through the lapping waves and start to walk up the beach - yes, you become suddenly aware that the fish tale has disappeared and you are back in human form. With a smile and a new magical energy surging through you, you continue to walk without looking back - knowing that you are rich, in all ways, and that the Universe is absolutely supporting that.

Chapter 7

Be the Magic

As we have discovered the elementals are the magic behind the workings of each of the elements that make this planet 'tick'. It is time to embrace the inspiration and enchantment of the faery world and integrate it with our everyday lives.

Humanity has tried to do things its way and, instead of leaving nature to do its 'thing' naturally, attempted to speed up the process by using man-made chemicals that are hampering the elementals doing their job effectively.

We are witnessing un-average amounts of tremors and earthquakes along the fault lines of the Earth, whilst the soil is corroded impeding healthy and plentiful growth of plants and crops. The water is suffering as oceans are filled with poisons that are killing the natural habitat of the seas. The air is polluted, causing extreme and severe weather changes and conditions. The fires of the Sun are at dangerous levels causing flares that affect all layers of the solar atmosphere.

The Earth, as a planet, is becoming very uncomfortable and we must take responsibility to ensure its, and our, future. All is not lost, however. For those who are awakening to the call of nature can feel their mystic-self stir from deep within. Glimmers of ancient memories surface recalling moonlit bathing in deep blue pools, weaving through paths of mystery through forests, feeling the magic of the Sun as it beams through the lush green leaves of the trees and dances through golden cornfields celebrating the harvest. To the elementals it was only yesterday when they played with you my friend. They miss you and the magic that you exude when you allow yourself be the free spirit you naturally are.

The world has changed and seems to spin at a much faster

pace, with high tech gadgets, transport and the like. To embrace the Faery Kingdom does not mean you have to lose everything and all that you know in this day and age. For when you recognise that the elementals are the beings who are the magic behind all that is alive on this wondrous planet and who work in conjunction with the elements that govern each and every one of us, you yourself are brought back into alignment with the natural world. In turn you will find that your own powerful manifestation and healing abilities are ignited enabling you to change how you experience life as you embrace the magic that is within and all around. And that is the way to bring the world back into balance.

The faeries are waiting in the waterfalls, the streams, in every meadow, garden and forest. They wait for you in the caves and hills, skies and oceans. They are present in every flower, each leaf, blade of grass and every rock and stone. Will you not acknowledge them and take a step sideways to become part of their magic? The true mystic keeps a foot in either world, for they know, and become part of, the reality of both. Time to introduce one of those worlds that has been hidden for too long now, into the other which has seemed to have lost its way without its magical counterpart.

The human body is made up of minerals, the same that are of Earth, 70% of our body is made up of water, our lungs fill with air 10 to 12 times per minute and we are ignited by the fire of spirit. Therefore we are made up from the basic elements meaning that we all have the energy of the elementals within us - which actually makes us all members of the Faery Realm!

Faery Incantation

'Faery seen or Faery Queen, Faery King or faery ring? Which calls to you, child of the dawn? One so young and yet was sworn, by the magical ones to keep on guard, the truth and wonder of the real back yard, where faeries play and invite you in, to the enchanting home

of their kingdom. When stars above twinkled their light, to shine your way through the mystical night, upon a ring of flowers you found, near the entrance to a faery mound. And as you bravely took that step, entwined within a world you wept. As new friends and old welcomed you in, to the enchanting home of their kingdom. Keep the light and shine it bright. Keep the truth with all your might. Keep the light and shine it bright, was the wisdom of that night. Faeries now seen and Faery Queens. Faery Kings and faery ring? Let the truth to all be now known, to those who will but listen and learn.'

World Healing Faery Meditation

Sitting comfortably, close your eyes, relax and take a few deep breaths. As you continue to breathe deeply visualise a thin circle of golden light forming around you. Now safe within this ethereal faery ring say aloud, or in your mind...

'Powerful faeries may we unite against all fears, let us shine our light and wrap it with love around the world, so healing's revealed and peace is unfurled.'

As faeries fly around you, become awash with the purest peace you have ever felt. Your heart begins to glow as you breathe in and out deeply. The heart-light expands and as it does so you become completely filled with this healing energy.

As the light continues to expand further it pushes down through the floor, forming a huge column of light that stretches all the way down through the ground. With the healing faeries to accompany you, you slide down this column of light and arrive safely in the centre of the Earth.

Gnomes, Elves and Salamanders stand around the hugest clear quartz crystal that has long points in each of the four directions of North, South, West and East. You, and the healing faeries, are invited to stand, like the others, with your arms outstretched and place your hands onto one the many facets of the mighty and powerful crystal.

As the peace light energy, that continues to run through you, fills the crystal you watch as it pulses and then spreads through each quartz point and out through the four directions into Mother Earth. The healing light spreads rapidly to every part of her, consuming and transmuting all negativity, fears and lower energies that the Earth Mother has had to endure over time.

The light expands up through the surface and then out into the oceans, cleansing and purifying. It flows across the lands, revitalising and nourishing.

Further up and out into the atmosphere the healing light of peace continues. It wraps itself around the planet's aura, like a blanket of healing, lifting Earth's frequency to that of a higher consciousness - awakening the hearts of all living beings to reveal a healed wholeness of peace and love.

Your work complete, you remove your hands from the crystal and are transported back up the column of light to where you started.

Take a deep breath and gently open your eyes. Receive the faeries heartfelt gratitude for your very real, and much needed, healing work that you have just given to the entire world.

Acknowledgements

To Barbara my beloved soul sister. Thank you for all your love, encouragement, support, great wisdom and for being my real life Faery God(dess) Mother! You are an inspiration and I am so blessed to be able to share the magical journey with you. Thank you from the very depths of my soul and heart for being in my life, for the fun and laughter, and for making all my dreams come true. I love you xxx

Kate (Kit Kat), thank you all your support, advice, passion and hard work that you have put into getting this book 'out there'. Immense gratitude and love to you for all you have done, and for all that you do.

Linda Ravenscroft, a big, big thank you for believing in the magic of this book by gifting me with the most beautiful faery artwork. Your great talent and faery connection is captured perfectly and I am so very honoured and blessed indeed that it graces the cover of this book.

Becca and Charlotte, thank you for the magical playtime we shared, as little girls, in Frilsham woods.

Thank you to Karen, Liz, Donna, Debbie, Doreen and Twinkle for the Faery share xxx and to Jamie, Carol and Sharon who have always been there.

About the Author

Flavia Kate Peters is a singer, writer, speaker, therapist and a natural mystic who connects with the ancient Deities of the Celtic British Isles and works closely with nature spirits. She offers readings and guidance as well as giving talks and workshops nationwide.

Flavia has always communed effortlessly with nature spirits and though she grew up heavily involved in the performing arts, she never lost her 'mystical connections'. Later she studied with Doreen Virtue, becoming her Angel Expert prodigy, but decided to explore further her love of all things pagan and more earthly.

She devotes her time now teaching others to work with the energies of Mother Nature, whilst still lending her expertise to many publications including *Spirit & Destiny*, *FAE Magazine* and presenting at major MBS events in the UK.

Flavia resides in Buxton, where she and shaman expert Barbara Meiklejohn-Free work under the popular 'Spirit Visions' banner.

www.flaviakatepeters.com

MOON
BOOKS

Moon Books invites you to begin or deepen your encounter with
Paganism, in all its rich, creative, flourishing forms.